Baptism According to Scripture

A Clear, Short, and Unfiltered Guide

Dr. Bobby Harrington

To our grandchildren: Ezra, Emma, Joshua, Elijah, Abigail, and one on the way. This teaching helped lead your great, great grandparents, your great grandparents, and your grandparents to surrender to Jesus as Savior and King—and we pray it helps lead you to do the same.

Contents

Introduction   5

1. By Jesus and his gospel, God offers us new life.   7
2. We receive new life through faith in Jesus.   11
3. Baptism expresses faith in Jesus for the forgiveness of sins.   13
4. Baptism expresses repentance.   17
5. Baptism imparts the indwelling Spirit.   21
6. Baptism is by immersion.   25
7. Baptism is for those old enough to express faith in Jesus.   29
8. Baptism is a commitment to discipleship in Jesus.   33
9. Baptism is the normative time of conversion in Scripture.   37
10. Baptism is an important practice in the local church.   45

Recommended Reading   48
Notes   49
About the Author   50

Introduction

I did not grow up in a Christian home, so when I made the decision as a young adult to trust and follow Jesus, I faced questions about baptism. Different church leaders, ministries, and Bible scholars guided me in conflicting ways. Is baptism by immersion, pouring, or sprinkling? Is it for babies or only for those old enough to decide for themselves? Is it an outward sign of an inward reality or a public demonstration of my faith, or is it more like a spiritual wedding ceremony resulting in a change of status between myself and God?

It took me some time to make sense of the different voices . . . until I made the decision to tune out all other voices and carefully listen to Scripture alone as my final authority.

You are likely reading this booklet because you have questions about baptism. Maybe you are confused about what the church you have been attending teaches on this topic. Or maybe someone has given you this booklet to help you gain a better understanding of baptism. It is natural to ask questions because what scripture teaches seems to be out of alignment with most evangelical or liturgical churches.

Here is an important note of caution. Churches, leaders, and their traditions—modern and ancient—may be your biggest barrier in the pursuit of clarity on baptism according to scripture. So I invite you to make the decision I made—to personally read and take Scripture alone as your truest guide and final authority (2 Timothy 3:16–4:4). Remind yourself, again and again, that all churches, all leaders, and all traditions (past, present, and future) are subject to God's Word. That goes for this booklet too—which is why its aim is to give a tour of what Scripture teaches about baptism, as clearly and simply as I'm able. The Scriptures are the "rule" or "ultimate standard" and "final authority" for God's people.[1] Nothing else should have *that role* in a Christian's life.

Here is another recommendation. Begin by reading through the book of Acts in the Bible—even before reading this booklet. It will not take you too long. Read it with one question in mind: *What does Acts teach about baptism?* Answer that question for yourself first.

Then pick up and read through this booklet. Work through the ten points. We will come back to the book of Acts at the end. As you read this booklet, consider the facts and discern whether what I have written aligns with God's Word. I have prayed for you, and I believe God will be with you.

The decision to trust and follow Jesus is the greatest decision a person will ever make. I believe this booklet will help you in understanding the role of baptism in that decision.

If you're seeking more detailed scholarly evidence and discussion, I've listed four recommended books at the end of this guide.

1.

By Jesus and his gospel, God offers us new life.

Before we can make sense of baptism, we need to see the big picture story of the Bible. The core story is what we call the "gospel," a word that means "good news." The gospel is the most important thing in the entire Bible because it tells us how God:

- Sent Jesus the Messiah to bring us into his kingdom
- Saves us from the penalty of our sins
- Gives us a right standing with him

> *The gospel is so amazing that it will change your life like nothing else in all creation.*

But first, to help us understand the gospel and why it is such good news, we need to understand the bad news.

The Bad News

In the beginning, God made a paradise for humans, a garden called Eden. But Genesis tells us that Adam and Eve disobeyed God through the devil's deceptive influence, and as a consequence, sin and brokenness entered into our world. The world continues to demonstrate the beauty of God's creation, but human sin and brokenness taint a part of everything in the world. Because God is holy—set apart as pure and perfectly good—human sin is a particularly huge problem. Human beings are now separated from God.

What do these realities look like in our lives?

- We care more about living our own way than we do about following God's way.
- We make selfish and sinful choices that hurt God, other people, and ourselves.
- The world has beauty, but brokenness and death now tarnish all of life.

Human beings are in trouble . . . we must be saved.

Without the good news of Jesus' gospel, we will remain separated from God.

- We will live without the blessing of knowing and walking with God in this life.
- After death, God will judge us for our sins.
- We will experience eternal punishment and be kept from heaven.

These truths are why we need help. We need good news.

The Gospel Is Good News

The good news is that God loves us so much he sent his Son, Jesus, to rescue us!

Jesus is the saving King promised in the Bible:

- Jesus came from heaven to earth to show us the way into God's kingdom.
- He lived a perfect life and taught us how to live.
- He died on the cross as an atonement for our sins.
- He was buried but rose from the dead three days later.
- He returned to heaven and now rules as King.
- One day, he will come back to punish those who continue to reject him and will make everything right for those who have faith in him.

This is why the gospel is such good news—Jesus has the power to take away all the bad, which came after the first humans disobeyed God in the garden of Eden, and he can bring us into his kingdom of love and righteousness.

The Gospel's Promises

Because of Jesus, God promises to restore all things. We can:

- Have our sins forgiven.
- Be part of God's kingdom now—living with blessings and purpose.
- Have God's Spirit live in us, helping and guiding us in this life.
- Experience a restoration of relationship with God and other people.
- Live with God forever in his eternal kingdom after we die.

God freely offers us new life through Jesus. We don't have to earn it, be good enough for it, or perform religious duties to get it. The Bible calls this grace—the unearned favor of God. Read and reflect on these beautiful scriptures:

> But when the kindness and love of God our Savior appeared, he saved us, not because of

GOD FREELY OFFERS US NEW LIFE THROUGH JESUS.

righteous things we had done, but because of his mercy . . . so that, having been justified by his grace, we might become heirs having the hope of eternal life. (Titus 3:4–5a, 7)

Therefore, if anyone is in Christ, the new creation has come: The old has gone, the new is here! All this is from God, who reconciled us to himself through Christ . . . God was reconciling the world to himself in Christ, not counting people's sins against them. . . . God made him who had no sin to be sin for us, so that in him we might become the righteousness of God. (2 Corinthians 5:17–19a, 21)

* * *

Under grace, God does not treat us as we deserve. Instead, he shows us infinite love and mercy. All praise and glory belong to God for the gospel.

Salvation is God's gift; it is a reflection of God's character, especially of his love for all human beings.

2.

We receive new life through faith in Jesus Christ.

Salvation, kingdom life, and right standing with God all come to us as the free gift of grace. But grace must be *accepted*. How? By placing our faith in Jesus. God is at work in our hearts to lead us into faith, but we must turn to him and respond to him. We must make the decision to place our faith in Jesus and give him our allegiance.[2]

Salvation is by grace *through* faith:

> For it is by grace you have been saved, through faith—and this not from yourselves, it is the gift of God—not by works, so that no one can boast. (Ephesians 2:8–9)

> For God so loved the world that he gave his one and only Son, that whoever believes in him shall not perish but have eternal life. (John 3:16)

God freely offers salvation to everyone who places their faith in Jesus and his gospel, no matter who we are or how badly we have lived (yes, the worst humans get saved the same way as the best humans). Everyone with faith gets the same right standing with God, in the same way. Right

EVERYONE WITH FAITH GETS THE SAME RIGHT STANDING WITH GOD.

standing with God is now based solely upon the goodness, mercy, and merit (or worth) of Jesus Christ and his gospel.

What Is Faith?

The faith we read about in the Bible is more than mere intellectual agreement or emotional warmth toward God. Faith is trusting and following God through Jesus. In other words, it is putting your trust in Jesus and giving your allegiance to him. Your faith can start small, but with God's help it is to grow into something living, active, and life-transforming. Through faith in Jesus, we learn to surrender our lives and come under the rule of God's kingdom in all things. God helps us do that by the power of his Spirit (2 Corinthians 3:3) and the help of the local church (Acts 2:42–46).

When you think of the word for "faith" or "belief" in the New Testament (they are the same root word in Greek), think of faith as *starting* with believing certain things about God and Jesus and pledging our allegiance to him—and then not stopping until it transforms everything about how we live.

Biblical faith is a faithful faith.

We know that we have come to know him if we keep his commands. Whoever says, "I know him," but does not do what he commands is a liar, and the truth is not in that person. (1 John 2:3-4)

The initial decision is as simple and straightforward as it is transformative. In its essential form, it is simply the decision and pledge to place our faith in Jesus and surrender to God through him.

Christianity, in its core essence begins with a simple faith that leads us into a transforming relationship with God.

3.

Baptism expresses faith in Jesus for the forgiveness of sins.

So far, we've looked at how God offers us new life through faith in Christ. But how does *baptism* connect with faith? Well, for starters, baptism is the way scripture teaches us to *express* our faith in Jesus as a personal decision. Before the early church leader Ananias baptized Saul/Paul, the notorious persecutor of Christians, here's what Ananias told him:

> Get up, be baptized and wash your sins away, *calling on his name.* (Acts 22:16b)

As Ananias described it, Paul was invited, in baptism, to call upon Jesus in faith. Ananias declared that baptism, as an expression of calling on Jesus' name, would wash Paul's sins away.

Let's look carefully at this teaching. Scripture shows us that God gives us baptism to express our faith in Jesus for the *forgiveness of sins.* Grace is God's part; faith is our part: baptism brings the two together as an expression of concrete belief and commitment.

GRACE IS GOD'S PART; FAITH IS OUR PART.

It is not about the water or the act itself, but the expression of one's *faith* in Jesus—as an act of trust and surrender so that through Jesus, God will save us.

Let's see what the following five passages from God's Word tell us about baptism:

> When the people heard this, they were cut to the heart and said to Peter and the other apostles, "Brothers, what shall we do?" Peter replied, "Repent and be baptized, every one of you, in the name of Jesus Christ for the forgiveness of your sins. And you will receive the gift of the Holy Spirit. (Acts 2:37–38)

> Then he said: "The God of our ancestors has chosen you to know his will and to see the Righteous One and to hear words from his mouth. . . . And now what are you waiting for? Get up, be baptized and wash your sins away, calling on his name." (Acts 22:14, 16)

> God waited patiently in the days of Noah while the ark was being built. In it only a few people, eight in all, were saved through water, and this water symbolizes baptism that now saves you also—not the removal of dirt from the body but the pledge of a clear conscience toward God. It saves you by the resurrection of Jesus Christ, who has gone into heaven and is at God's right hand—with angels, authorities and powers in submission to him. (1 Peter 3:20b–22)

> So in Christ Jesus you are all children of God through faith, for all of you who were baptized into Christ have clothed yourselves with Christ. There is neither Jew nor Gentile, neither slave nor free, nor is there male and female, for you are all one in Christ Jesus. (Galatians 3:26–28)

> Having been buried with him in baptism, in which you were also raised with him through your faith in the working of God, who raised him from the dead. (Colossians 2:12)

These five passages are significant. Each relates baptism to one's personal expression of faith. In Acts 2:37–38, the apostle Peter told the people to be baptized "in the name of Jesus Christ for the forgiveness of your sins." The phrase "in the name of Jesus Christ," in the Greek text, is an expression of reliance on Jesus Christ for the purpose of forgiveness of sins. The British scholar I. Howard Marshall's words help us to understand this passage:

> However precisely the phrase be understood, it conveys the thought that the person being baptized enters into *allegiance to* Jesus. . . . Thus, Christian baptism was an expression of faith and commitment to Jesus as Lord.[3]

First Peter 3:21 teaches that baptism brings salvation because it is "the pledge of a good conscience toward God." The Greek can also be translated as an "appeal to God for a good conscience." The idea is that, in baptism, you appeal to God, expressing faith in the risen Christ to save you from your sins, and it will give you a clear conscience with God.

According to Galatians 3:26–27, the decision to be baptized is a concrete commitment to be clothed with Christ. And Colossians 2:12 powerfully reminds us that baptism's benefits come "through your faith in the working of God." All of these passages demonstrate that the act of baptism is not a human work, but the ceremony God gave us to be our expression of faith in Jesus.

THE DECISION TO BE BAPTIZED IS A CONCRETE COMMITMENT.

Think about the analogy of a wedding ceremony: The groom gives his heart to the bride, and the bride gives her heart to the groom. Each part of the marriage ceremony can be significant, but the commitment of personal faithfulness to each other from the heart is the most important part of the ceremony and the foundational basis of the marital union.

By way of analogy, in baptism, we express our faith in Jesus, pledging our allegiance to him. Just as a wedding ceremony is a covenant-making moment between a husband and wife, these passages show baptism to be a covenant-making moment between a sinner turning to Jesus in faith and God, who forgives that sinner based on his grace.

Baptism marks the turning point.

By baptism, we concretely place our faith in Jesus for the forgiveness of sins. Again, consider Acts 2:38b:

> Be baptized, every one of you, in the name of Jesus Christ for the forgiveness of your sins. And you will receive the gift of the Holy Spirit.

This text is clear, at baptism, God forgives us and gives us his Spirit. Again, the baptism ceremony is the method God designed to express our faith and commitment to him in a concrete moment.

Baptism is the ceremony, and personal faith in Jesus and his gospel are at the heart of the ceremony.

4.

Baptism expresses repentance.

You likely noticed another word used in conjunction with baptism. It is the word "repent." We cannot understand baptism in scripture apart from understanding "repentance." What exactly is repentance, and how does it relate to faith and baptism?

The Greek word used in the New Testament for "repentance" (*metanoia*) literally means "to have another mind," or "a change of mind." It is a decision to make a change, to turn around and go a different direction. Thus, Christian repentance is a necessary and natural part of placing personal faith in Christ, choosing to follow him and his way over your own way and desires.

Through repentance, you both renounce your sin and selfish ways and choose Jesus as Savior, Lord, and King (the alternative to sin and selfish ways). The Bible is clear: repentance is at the heart of the Christian faith. We cannot properly embrace Jesus Christ through faith unless we simultaneously pledge to turn from our sinful ways in repentance. God offers us

BY FAITH, WE MUST BE WILLING TO TURN FROM OUR SINFUL LIFESTYLES.

healing from our sin, but by faith, we must be willing to turn from our sinful lifestyles.

The faith taught in Scripture is like a coin. One side of the coin is repentance from sin; the other is allegiance to Jesus and his ways. We can't turn toward allegiance to Jesus unless we simultaneously turn away from our sinful ways.

> Repent, then, and turn to God, so that your sins may be wiped out, that times of refreshing may come from the Lord. (Acts 3:19)
>
> I have declared to both Jews and Greeks that they must turn to God in repentance and have faith in our Lord Jesus. (Acts 20:21)
>
> First to those in Damascus, then to those in Jerusalem and in all Judea, and then to the Gentiles, I preached that they should repent and turn to God and demonstrate their repentance by their deeds. (Acts 26:20)

One way of summarizing these passages is to say that repentance is an integral part of saving faith in Jesus Christ, essential for those who wish to receive his salvation.

In Scripture, both faith and repentance are pulled together in baptism.

Baptism makes faith and repentance a concrete commitment to God.

> When the people heard this, they were cut to the heart and said to Peter and the other apostles, "Brothers, what shall we do?" Peter replied, "Repent and be baptized, every one of you, in the name of Jesus Christ for the forgiveness of your sins. And you will receive the gift of the Holy Spirit." (Acts 2:37–38)

It makes sense that both repentance and faith are brought together in baptism when you consider what it reenacted in baptism: death and resurrection.

The book of Romans includes a lengthy section describing how as Christians, we pledge ourselves to turn from our sin to live God's way. The

Faith and repentance are pulled together in baptism.

apostle Paul uses "death" to help us understand what he's saying: when Christians come to faith in Christ, they pledge to die to the controlling influence of their sinful lifestyles. Scripture ties repentance as "death to sin" directly to baptism.

> Or don't you know that all of us who were baptized into Christ Jesus were baptized into his death? We were therefore buried with him through baptism into death in order that, just as Christ was raised from the dead through the glory of the Father, we too may live a new life. (Romans 6:3–5)

In this way, Christians naturally looked back to their baptism as a turning point in their lives: the end of the old way and the beginning of God's new way. In Scripture, God promises to help those who repent through the power of his Holy Spirit. Also, God teaches us that we need help from other disciples and the local church to live a life of repentance (Matthew 28:19–20; Acts 2:42). Repentance means change, a big change, especially for adults who have established sinful lifestyle patterns and then they come to Christ. But God is faithful and will help everyone who turns to him.

So when you're making the decision to be baptized, spend time thinking and praying about what God teaches about sin and the sinful habits. You will need others to help disciple you and show you how to give up these patterns. Confess and acknowledge your decision to turn from these behaviors. Most importantly, trust God to help you as you learn to personally rely upon him daily.

In baptism, we repent and turn away from sinful lifestyle choices; it is surrendering your heart to God and pledging to him—that with his help, you will change your ways.

5.

Baptism imparts the indwelling Spirit.

So let's summarize what we've said so far. God offers us new life in Christ. To accept that offer, we repent of our sinful ways and place our faith in Jesus to save us from our sins and give us a new life. But how and when? Faith and repentance come together in baptism.

And then from there, we simply try harder to live a new life, right? Is that what happens after baptism? Thankfully, *that's not* the rest of the story. God promises to give us a helper to walk with us and live inside us—a helper who is none other than God himself.

GOD GIVES US A HELPER TO WALK WITH US AND LIVE INSIDE US.

The indwelling of the Holy Spirit is the distinguishing mark in Scripture that delineates a Christian from a non-Christian—the saved from the lost.

> When you believed, you were marked in him with a seal, the promised Holy Spirit, who is a deposit guaranteeing our inheritance until the redemption of those who are God's possession—to the praise of his glory. (Ephesians 1:13b–14)

Again, Acts 2:38 teaches that the Spirit of God is given to the believer at the point of water baptism:

> Peter replied, "Repent and be baptized, every one of you, in the name of Jesus Christ for the forgiveness of your sins. And you will receive the gift of the Holy Spirit."

The reality that the Spirit comes to dwell within us at the point of conversion is described in synonymous ways in the Bible, such as the following:

- "God . . . showed that he accepted them by giving the Holy Spirit to them. (Acts 15:8)
- The "Spirit is . . . **poured out** on us generously through Jesus Christ our Savior, so that . . . we might become heirs having the hope of eternal life." (Titus 3:5–7)
- "The Holy Spirit had been poured out even on Gentiles . . . . They have received the Holy Spirit just as we have." (Acts 10:45–47)

WHEN YOU SURRENDER TO CHRIST, YOU ARE BAPTIZED BY THE HOLY SPIRIT.

All these expressions are different ways of describing the indwelling gift of the Holy Spirit, establishing a person as a child of God and empowering them for godly living. Thus, when you surrender your life to Christ, you are "baptized by the Holy Spirit" and receive "the indwelling of the Holy Spirit." In 1 Corinthians 12:13, the apostle Paul describes it succinctly:

> For we were all baptized by one Spirit so as to form one body—whether Jews or Gentiles, slave or free—and we were all given the one Spirit to drink.

It is helpful to think about baptism in two parts: the external water and the internal Spirit. The following passages are helpful on this point.

He saved us through the washing of rebirth and renewal by the Holy Spirit, whom he poured out on us generously through Jesus Christ our Savior, so that, having been justified by his grace, we might become heirs having the hope of eternal life. (Titus 3:5b–7)

But you were washed, you were sanctified, you were justified in the name of the Lord Jesus Christ and by the Spirit of our God. (1 Corinthians 6:11b)

Jesus answered, "Very truly I tell you, no one can enter the kingdom of God unless they are born of water and the Spirit. (John 3:5)

Again, according to Scripture, baptism is the point at which we receive the Holy Spirit. This point is punctuated in Acts 19:1–7 when the apostle Paul encounters disciples who had not yet received the Holy Spirit. They had been baptized by John the Baptist—a baptism of repentance—which God intended for bringing about the forgiveness of sins. But God did not intend for John's baptism to impart the Holy Spirit.

[Paul] asked them, "Did you receive the Holy Spirit when you believed?" They answered, "No, we have not even heard that there is a Holy Spirit." So Paul asked, "Then what baptism did you receive?" "John's baptism," they replied. Paul said, "John's baptism was a baptism of repentance. He told the people to believe in the one coming after him, that is, in Jesus." On hearing this, they were baptized in the name of the Lord Jesus. (Acts 19:2–5)

This helps us to understand how John the Baptist's baptism was different from baptism into Jesus. John's baptism focused on repentance, but it did not teach people to rely on Jesus' sacrifice of atonement because Jesus had not yet died during John's ministry. John's baptism was only meant for a temporary period. So after Jesus' death, burial, resurrection, and ascension to God's right hand in heaven, even those baptized by John had to be baptized into Jesus. This is when they received the indwelling Spirit.

God's Word teaches us that we can rely on him to give us the Holy Spirit as his indwelling presence when we are baptized into Christ.

In baptism, the Holy Spirit takes up residence within us. He is God's empowering presence within.

6.

Baptism is by immersion.

The New Testament was written in the Greek language. The Greek word used in the New Testament for baptism is *baptizō*. It means "to dip, plunge, or to immerse."[4] If God had wanted us to follow a different method of baptism, then the New Testament would have used different words to describe the act of baptism. If God had meant to say "pour," he could have used *ekcheō*, which means "to pour out." If he wanted to say "sprinkle," he would have used *rhantizō*, which means "to sprinkle." God intended for the writers of Scripture to describe immersion because the word used is *baptizō*.[5]

What's helpful is that even without knowing that the word for baptism in the original text was *baptizō*, we can still determine what baptism is by the descriptions of baptism in the New Testament. One of the clearest examples is found in Romans 6.

Paul described baptism as a drama with three distinct acts:

1. The first act was a death. When a person went into the water, they pledged to identify themselves with Christ's death (Romans 6:3).

2. The second act was a burial. In this water burial, a person reenacted the burial of Christ (Romans 6:4).
3. The third act was a resurrection. In coming out of the water, a person was raised to live a new kind of life (Romans 6:4–5).

Whenever a person was baptized, there was a reenactment of the death, burial, and resurrection of Jesus. No other action communicates this rich biblical principle except immersion.

> Or don't you know that all of us who were baptized into Christ Jesus were baptized into his death? We were therefore buried with him through baptism into death in order that, just as Christ was raised from the dead through the glory of the Father, we too may live a new life. For if we have been united with him in a death like his, we will certainly also be united with him in a resurrection like his. (Romans 6:3–5)

The picture these verses paint for us is that baptism—as a death, a burial, and then a raising up with Christ—is an immersion.

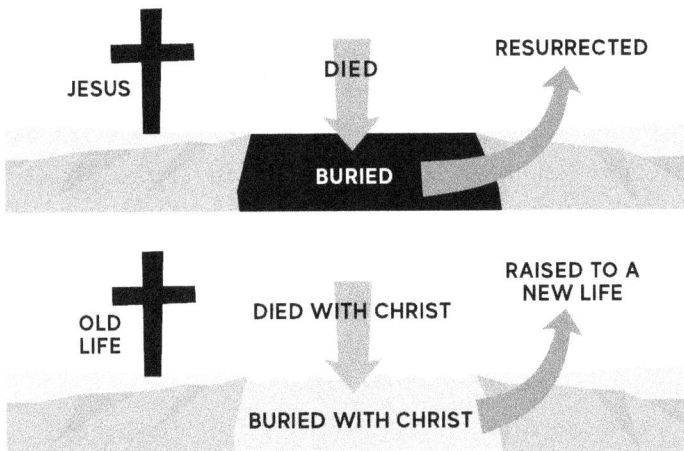

The same point is made in Colossians 2:12 when the apostle Paul describes the physical act of baptism as a burial.

Baptism is an immersion that re-enacts the death, burial, and raising of Jesus.

Having been buried with him in baptism, in which you were also raised with him through your faith in the working of God, who raised him from the dead.

It would be unwise to look upon water immersion simply as a cultural practice used to express faith in Christ in the first century.

Water immersion is a picture of our sins being washed away (Acts 22:16).

Romans 6 shows us that the meaning of the commitment to follow Christ is expressed in the method used to make the commitment.

Baptism thus becomes a patternmaker for the rest of our lives, showing what lies at the heart of conversion and discipleship—the constant dying to self and rising with Christ (Romans 6:17).

Baptism pictures the gospel: by water immersion, we reenact the death, burial, and resurrection of Jesus.

7.

Baptism is for those old enough to express faith in Jesus.

If you carefully investigate the traditions of the various streams of Christianity, you'll find several schools of thought on when a person is ready for baptism. Some think infants can be baptized, while others do not. Some think that if infants are dedicated (e.g., at a special ceremony at church), they are as good as baptized. Scripture has specific teachings concerning baptism and will both guide us and bring clarity on the age for baptism question.

First, as we've seen, Scripture tells us that a person must believe in Jesus Christ to be baptized. Let's look at a few examples. The apostle Peter described baptism as the point at which a person was saved. This is because in baptism, a person made a "pledge of a clear conscience toward God" (1 Peter 3:21; or made an "appeal to God for a good conscience" (New Revised Standard Version); or, as in the words of Ananias to Paul, we call on Jesus' name in baptism (Acts 22:16). In Colossians 2:12, the apostle Paul describes baptism as the time we are *raised with him through your faith* in the working of God, who raised him from the dead." These scriptures and others teach that to be baptized, a person must believe in Jesus, pledge a good conscience, call on his name, and put their faith in the working of God through baptism.

Second, as we've also seen, baptism is a pledge of personal repentance. On the day of Pentecost, Peter told three thousand people they were to "repent and be baptized" (Acts 2:38). The promises of the gift of the Holy Spirit and the forgiveness of sins were available *only to those who could repent and be baptized*. Thus, according to these scriptures, baptism requires a person to be at a point of moral development in which they realize they are sinners in need of a savior and are willing to turn from a sinful life (Romans 6:1–6).

BAPTISM IS A PLEDGE OF PERSONAL REPENTANCE.

These teachings contrast with the Old Testament, where infants were added to the faith community when they were circumcised shortly after birth. The New Testament is different: baptism is based on a person's faith. Unlike God's covenant with Israel, you are *not physically born* into Jesus' kingdom. You can only come into the kingdom *by a personal decision to place your faith in Jesus Christ.*[6]

Notice how the apostle Paul contrasted the circumcision of babies in the Old Testament with the expression of faith through baptism in the New Testament:

> In him you were also circumcised with a circumcision not performed by human hands. Your whole self ruled by the flesh [was put off when you were circumcised by] Christ, having been buried with him in baptism, in which **you were also raised with him through your faith in the working of God**, who raised him from the dead. When you were dead in your sins and in the uncircumcision of your flesh, God made you] alive with Christ. He forgave us all our sins. (Colossians 2:11–13)

In this text, Paul points out that baptism was like circumcision—through it, people were brought into a covenant relationship with God. But unlike circumcision, the one being baptized *expressed faith in the power of God.*

These truths provide the background that explains why infant baptism did not become a common practice until over three hundred years after the writing of the New Testament.[7] The first time it comes up is about 125 years after the New Testament documents were completed. The influential leader Tertullian opposed it, noting that young children must first develop faith.

Some will offer inferences to support infant baptism in Scripture. For example, there's the analogy of baptism to circumcision, and there is the mention of entire households receiving baptism. Infant baptism is not based on Scripture, but on the development of later human traditions. By way of summary, here are some perspectives which keep us grounded in the teaching of scripture:

INFANT BAPTISM IS NOT BASED ON SCRIPTURE.

1. Infants cannot repent and place their faith in Jesus, which is required for baptism according to the New Testament.
2. There are no passages that explicitly teach infant baptism.
3. Household conversions do not provide explicit examples of infant baptism - when we carefully examine "household" conversions, the text points us to extended families and friends, with an emphasis on their faith and no mention of infants (see Acts 10:24 and 15:7–9).
4. Circumcision is not parallel to infant water baptism, but to the indwelling of the Holy Spirit—given based on faith (see Romans 2:29).
5. The baptism of believers is the only sure and clear teaching of Scripture.

Again, all scholars agree that baptism that expresses faith is grounded in Scripture. Those who practice infant baptism do so based on their best understanding, but when pressed, it's based on human tradition more than clear scriptural teaching. That's why following what's clear in God's Word is the most solid footing.

> ***We dedicate our children to God when they are born, but they are born again when they personally dedicate themselves to God by faith in Jesus Christ in baptism.***

8.

Baptism is a commitment to discipleship in Jesus.

What is the point of a wedding ceremony? The wedding ceremony is best understood as enacting a lifelong covenant commitment. Couples partake in the ceremony with the intention that the covenant they make will last for a lifetime.

The same thing is true in baptism. Jesus teaches that baptism marks our transition into the new life in his kingdom, where we will live as his faithful disciples until the end of life. Understood this way, baptism is not the finish line, but the starting line. Jesus doesn't just save us; he wants to transform us into his image by our obedience so we become more and more like him. Look at Jesus' final words in Matthew 28:19–20:

BAPTISM IS NOT THE FINISH LINE, BUT THE STARTING LINE.

> Therefore go and make disciples of all nations, baptizing them in the name of the Father and of the Son and of the Holy Spirit, and teaching them to obey everything I have commanded you. And surely I am with you always, to the very end of the age.

33

In the original Greek text, Jesus gave only one imperative command to his disciples in his Great Commission: *make disciples.*[8] He added three phrases to show how we are to make disciples: we *go*, we *baptize*, and we *teach obedience*. In the Great Commission, baptism happens "in the name of the Father and of the Son and of the Holy Spirit" (Matthew 28:19b). The act of baptism transfers us into the possession of the Father, Son, and Holy Spirit.

These verses describe baptism as a commitment to discipleship in Jesus—the process of being progressively transformed into his image. Coming out of baptism we learn to *obey everything* Jesus *commanded* as his disciple (Matthew 28:20). We can't do that on our own—we need the people of God, the Word of God, the mission of God, and especially the Spirit of God. That's why Jesus promises to be with us, shaping us into his image until the "end of the age" (Matthew 28:20).

The apostle Paul makes this same point in various places, including Romans 6:4:

> We were therefore buried with him through baptism into death in order that, just as Christ was raised from the dead through the glory of the Father, we too may live a new life.

And in Galatians 2:20, Paul describes the reality of this commitment:

> I have been crucified with Christ and I no longer live, but Christ lives in me. The life I now live in the body, I live by faith in the Son of God, who loved me and gave himself for me.

The focus on committing ourselves to discipleship in Jesus through baptism is also a good way to sum up the other parts of baptism we discussed earlier.

- Baptism is about expressing faith—it is to trust and commit to follow Jesus, giving him our allegiance, loyalty, and faithfulness (Galatians 3:26–27).
- Baptism is about repentance—we turn *toward* Jesus as we commit to *turn away* from our flesh and sinful behaviors (Acts 2:38).

Rising out of baptism we learn to *obey everything Jesus commanded.*

- Baptism is about the Holy Spirit—God promises to come and dwell within us, to empower and help us follow his ways, when we place our faith in Jesus in baptism (Titus 3:5).
- Baptism is about entry into the kingdom of God—we are literally transferred from the kingdom of darkness into the kingdom of light (Colossians 1:13), when we are born again through Jesus (John 3:5).

ALL WHO RESPOND TO SALVATION IN BAPTISM ARE CALLED TO DISCIPLESHIP.

Baptism marks a big change in our lives. All who respond to salvation in baptism are freely saved and called to discipleship—no exceptions, no excuses (Mark 8:34–38; 1 Corinthians 15:1–8).

Baptism is about crossing the line into the greatest adventure on planet earth—living everyday as a disciple of King Jesus.

9.

Baptism is the normative time of conversion in Scripture.

Passages like Ephesians 4:3–6 describe core or elementary teachings of the faith which form the basis of our unity. The apostle Paul teaches us that we should "make every effort to keep the unity of the Spirit through the bond of peace" in verse three. He then goes on to tell us that the local church is built on seven core elements of the faith:

> One body and one Spirit, just as you were called to one hope when
> you were called; one Lord, one faith, one baptism; one God and
> Father of all, who is over all and through all and in all.

Based upon what we have seen so far, we would naturally expect baptism to be on this list. It ties in with the essential elements of the faith described in related passages like Acts 2:26–42, Galatians 3:23–29, Matthew 28:18–20, etc.

Yet this can create problems with the experience of many believers and Christians in history. How can we uphold baptism as the way to express faith in Jesus for the forgiveness of sins, while also recognizing God's work among other devout believers who have not followed this teaching? This question can be especially difficult when it seems clear that they have the indwelling Spirit. You may be a person reading this booklet and you have not been baptized as we have described, but you believe by personal experience that the Holy Spirit lives within you or came to live within you before your baptism (Romans 8:16–17).

And what about the *sinner's prayer* or asking Jesus into your heart? Many Christian leaders encourage us to say a prayer to express our faith, and they tell us we will get saved by that prayer. Maybe you prayed that prayer and placed your faith in Jesus at that moment. It can be difficult to put these experiences together with what this booklet has been teaching.

When we put together all that Scripture teaches about baptism, it is most accurate to describe baptism as the *normative* way in Scripture to express faith in Jesus for salvation. The expression "normative way in Scripture" is key. If you read through the book of Acts, you will see that there is a clear norm when it comes to baptism—but there are also a few variations. There were circumstances where God worked things out differently when it came to the gospel coming to two non-Jewish groups for the first time: the Samaritans in Acts 8 (i.e., the Holy Spirit was given after baptism) and Cornelius and his household in Acts 10 and 11 (i.e., the Holy Spirit came upon them before baptism).

> **BAPTISM IS THE *NORMATIVE* WAY IN SCRIPTURE TO EXPRESS FAITH FOR SALVATION.**

Here are a cluster of six key insights that help us to see baptism as the scriptural norm, while we acknowledge deviations from the scriptural norm and seek to honestly face good questions that arise from what has been taught so far.

1. Scripture, not experience, should be our final authority.

We must not deny experiences, but we should let Scripture interpret our experiences. Factually, the sinner's prayer as the moment of conversion is not found in Scripture, nor do we see it used as such in the early church or throughout church history. It was popularized by the evangelist Billy

Graham and Campus Crusade in the mid-1900s, and it became standard practice among evangelicals only around that time.

Many point to Romans 10:9–10 for support of the sinner's prayer. This passage describes the benefit of believing with your heart and confessing with your mouth.

> If you declare with your mouth, "Jesus is Lord," and believe in your heart that God raised him from the dead, you will be saved. For it is with your heart that you believe and are justified, and it is with your mouth that you profess your faith and are saved.

However, this passage actually doesn't describe someone being led to say the sinner's prayer. Instead, Romans 10:9–10 more likely describes a declaration of faith that was part of the baptism ceremony in the early church. Romans 6 comes before Romans 10 and shows, in keeping with the rest of the New Testament, that baptism was the time when the believers in Rome entered into the benefits of Jesus' death (see Romans 6:3–4). When standing in the water, just before baptism, someone about to be baptized said, "Jesus is Lord!" It was like a bride or groom declaring their vows as a part of the wedding ceremony. People declared their faith in Jesus just before they were immersed in the water.

2. Baptismal regeneration is not biblical.

"Baptismal regeneration" is the doctrine that the act of baptism, even apart from personal faith, brings salvation. This is contrary to Scripture, and it should be obvious that this booklet does not teach baptismal regeneration. When Protestant Christianity emerged in the early 1500s, there was a strong rejection of the doctrine of baptismal regeneration, which was the doctrine of the Roman Catholic and Eastern Orthodox churches. These churches teach that salvation is granted to infants, who do not have personal faith, when they are baptized. This teaching contradicts passages like Ephesians 2:8–9, John 3:16, and Colossians 2:12, which teach us that *a person is saved by grace through personal faith.*

Yet, in their rightful rejection of baptismal regeneration, many Protestant groups overreacted to the extent of teaching that baptism has nothing or little to do with the conversion process. They began to interpret baptism as a mere symbol or a sign of salvation already received. Others saw it as nothing more than a public demonstration of faith, not as a covenant-making moment.

The Protestants were right in affirming that salvation comes by grace through faith (Romans 3:23–25). However, they often went too far the other way by minimizing baptism's role as the God-ordained way to express saving faith.

3. God gives salvation and the Spirit as he sees fit.

I would urge caution when it comes to dismissing the millions upon millions of otherwise faithful believers throughout history—and in our world today—who did not know to practice baptism as the correct expression of repentance and faith in response to the gospel in conversion. They were unfortunately taught by teachers overly influenced by the lenses of human traditions or theological bias.

At the same time, we can be grateful when Jesus and the gospel were still present in their teachings. Many of these believers have shown deep faith in Jesus and seem to exhibit clear evidence of the Holy Spirit's presence in their lives. The point about the Holy Spirit is worth highlighting because, according to God's Word, the presence of the Holy Spirit distinguishes those who are truly saved from those who are lost. Ephesians 1:13–14 teaches that the Holy Spirit is the true mark or seal of salvation:

> And you also were included in Christ when you heard the message of truth, the gospel of your salvation. When you believed, you were marked in him with a seal, the promised Holy Spirit, who is a deposit guaranteeing our inheritance until the redemption of those who are God's possession—to the praise of his glory.

The presence of the Holy Spirit distinguishes those who are truly saved.

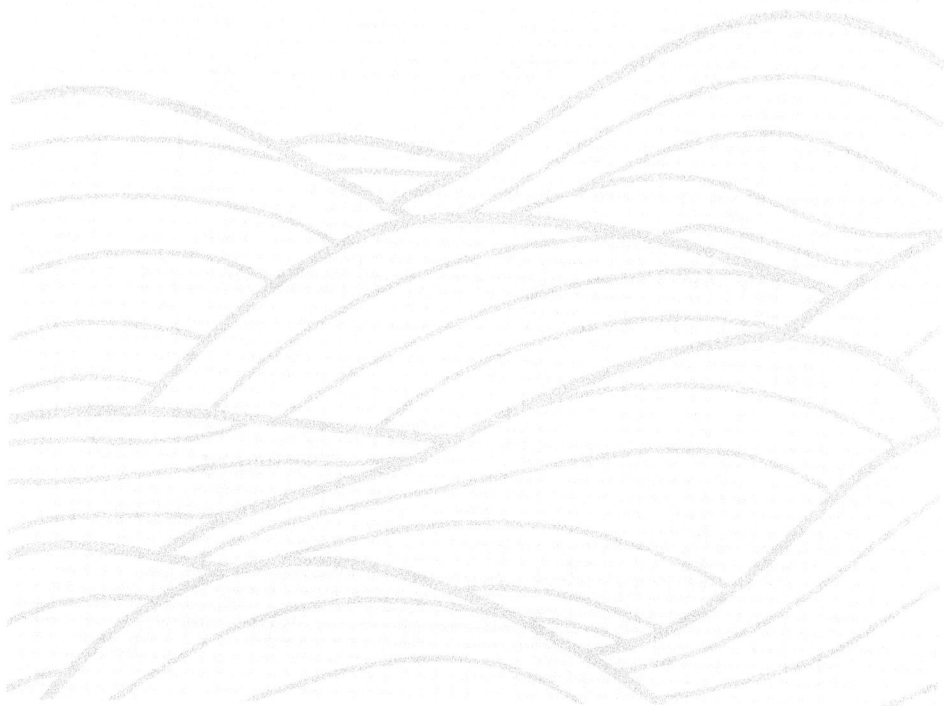

This is a crucial point for consideration. You will meet people who were not properly baptized, yet they have true faith in Jesus, live for him, and bear the fruit of the Holy Spirit—manifested in love for God, transformation into the image of Christ, and a life of true discipleship in Jesus. Surely this formation is by the indwelling Spirit. Is it possible that God, who knows the heart, saved them? Yes, I personally believe that God, seeing their genuine faith in Jesus and his gospel, granted them his Holy Spirit (Acts 15:8).

God's saving power is not limited by an imperfect understanding or practice of baptism.

We can believe that God is merciful, kind, and gracious to those who sincerely surrender to Jesus in faith, to the best of their understanding, while we still uphold baptism in the normative way.

4. Baptism is not a work.

The Jewish Christians in the book of Galatians thought God would save them because of what they did when they kept the ceremonial laws. They tried to be right with God based upon their works. The apostle Paul called it a different (false) gospel (Galatians 1:6–9). Scripture clearly teaches that we are saved by grace through faith, not by works (Ephesians 2:8–9).

Yet some teachers today turn anything you do to respond in faith to the gospel into a work – even repentance and confession. But that is not in keeping with Scripture. We need some way to express our decision to turn to Jesus and place our faith in him. That is how the tradition of the sinner's prayer arose. But Scripture provides us with a simple ceremony. The way God teaches us to express our faith it is not through a prayer, but through baptism. Baptism embodies the gospel, as we reenact Christ's death, burial, and resurrection by faith (Romans 6:2–5).

Instead of being a work we do, baptism is a divine gift we receive. We are not the agents in baptism; God is. We don't "do" baptism; we confess our faith and rely on Jesus as we are lowered into the water. We are the recipients of grace by faith in baptism.

5. God is not bound by baptism, but we are bound to uphold it as our norm.

Those who teach God's Word are bound to faithfully uphold its teaching. The whole New Testament, particularly the book of Acts, consistently emphasizes that baptism is the God-ordained means for expressing personal faith in Jesus at conversion and for entrance into the Christian life. We who know the truth are bound by God's Word to faithfully uphold this normative teaching on baptism.

Again, we can accept that God transcends the norms of the methodology he established because he alone knows the heart (1 Samuel 16:7; Acts 15:8). That is his prerogative, not ours. We must be careful that we do not presume to be God.

God is God, and he can and will save those with faith when and where he pleases. But God's prerogative is distinct from the ordinary means by which he wills to save us and that he himself instituted through the teaching of the apostles in Scripture. We need to uphold scriptural norms about baptism while making room for God to work outside of those norms when he so chooses.

6. Even if you believe you have the Spirit apart from baptism, it is time to be baptized.

The story of Cornelius in the Bible shows that anyone who has reason to believe they have received the Holy Spirit apart from baptism should still adhere to the biblical command to be baptized. Acts 10:47–48 describes this exact situation when Cornelius and his household received the Spirit to demonstrate that God accepted non-Jews who believed in the gospel. They received the Spirit apart from their baptism, but Peter told them to be baptized.

Then Peter said, "Surely no one can stand in the way of their being baptized with water. They have received the Holy Spirit just as we have." So he ordered that they be baptized in the name of Jesus Christ. (Acts 10:47–48a)

We should follow Peter and insist on the same practice today.

In this way, Jesus' baptism can also be an example. He did not need forgiveness but was baptized to fulfill all righteousness (Matthew 3:15). In a similar way, those convinced they have the Spirit apart from baptism should still be baptized to fulfill all the righteous teachings of God.

As mentioned earlier, baptism is one of seven pillars of unity for God's people, as outlined in Ephesians 4:3–6. The early Christians treated baptism as a vital and nonnegotiable component of conversion when they taught God's ways. We should do the same today.

Baptism is the normative way God intends for us to express faith in Jesus for the forgiveness of sins.

10.

Baptism is an important practice for the local church.

Every gospel-centered, Scripture-based, local church should uphold the practice of baptism according to the Scriptures. Let's look again at what Acts 2:38–41 teaches:

> Peter replied, "Repent and be baptized, every one of you, in the name of Jesus Christ for the forgiveness of your sins. And you will receive the gift of the Holy Spirit. The promise is for you and your children and for all who are far off—for all whom the Lord our God will call." (Acts 2:38–39)

EVERY GOSPEL-CENTERED, SCRIPTURE-BASED CHURCH SHOULD UPHOLD THE PRACTICE OF BAPTISM.

Peter warned and pleaded with the crowd that had gathered: *"Save yourselves from this corrupt generation"* (Acts 2:40b). Those who accepted his message were baptized, and Scripture tells us that about three thousand were added to their number that day.

In the introduction to this booklet, I encouraged everyone to read the entire book of Acts in the Bible. My hope was for you to have the raw experience of simply reading about baptism in the early church. It is personally very convicting.

So we come back to Acts as we end this booklet. The teaching in Acts 2:38–39 provides us with an important perspective on why baptism should be the norm or standard for how we teach people to respond in repentant faith to Jesus and the gospel today.

1. These verses describe the role of baptism on the day of Pentecost, which was the founding day of the church. It is an important day for clarity.
2. The words and meaning of these verses are a clear guide: baptism as an expression of faith in Jesus (literally baptism "on his name") is *for* the forgiveness of sins and results in the Holy Spirit coming to live in us.[9]
3. Acts 2:39 presents baptism and its promises as the standard for conversion and the expansion of church until the end of history. The text says the promises of forgiveness and the gift of the Holy Spirit are "for you and your children and for all who are far off—for all whom the Lord our God will call." That includes us!
4. These verses set the stage and function as the standard for all subsequent conversions in the book of Acts (and the New Testament as a whole). The following chart is a helpful tool to look at conversions in Acts.[10]

Text	Heard	Believed	Repented	Baptized	Holy Spirit	Saved
Pentecost Acts 2:14–41	Heard 2:37	Believed 2:37	Repented 2:38	Baptized 2:41	At Immersion 2:38	Remission of Sins 2:38
Samaria Acts 8:5–13	Heard 8:12	Believed 8:13		Baptized 8:12–13	After Immersion 8:15–17	
Eunuch Acts 8:35–39	Heard 8:35	Believed 8:36		Baptized 8:38–39		Rejoicing 8:39
Saul Acts 9:1–18; 22:1–16; 26:9–18	Heard 9:4–6	Believed 22:10	Repented 9:9	Baptized 9:18	At Immersion 9:17–18	Washed Away Sins 22:16
Cornelius Acts 10:34–48 11:4–18; 15:7–11	Heard 10:44; 11:14	Believed 10:43	Repented 11:18	Baptized 10:48	Before Immersion 10:46–47	Purified Hearts 15:9
Lydia Acts 16:13–15	Heard 16:14	Believed 16:14		Baptized 16:15		
Jailor Acts 16:30–34	Heard 16:32	Believed 16:31	Repented 16:33	Baptized 16:33		Rejoiced 16:34
Corinthians Acts 18:8	Heard 18:8	Believed 18:8		Baptized 18:8		
Ephesian Disciples Acts 19:1–7	Heard 19:2	Believed 19:2		Baptized 19:5	After Immersion 19:6	

5. The teaching of this booklet – that baptism is to express faith for the forgiveness of sins – was also the teaching of the earliest Christians after the apostles died. For over three hundred years, the earliest church fathers taught what this booklet teaches. They also emphasized Acts 2:38, as reflected in the Nicene Creed of 381 C.E. which states:

We confess one baptism for the forgiveness of sins.

Notes

1. See Anthony Lane's helpful and nuanced work on t scriptura? Making Sense of a Post-Reformation Slogaı thwaite & D. F. Wright (eds.), *A Pathway into the Hoı* Rapids, MI: Eerdmans, 1994), 297–327.
2. 1 John 2:20, 27; Acts 7:51
3. I. Howard Marshall, *Acts* in Tyndale New Testame (Grand Rapids, MI: Eerdmans, 1980), 81.
4. For more information see *A Greek-English Lexicon ı ment and Other Early Christian Literature*, Walter Bau William Danker, 3rd ed. (Chicago: University of Chiı Also, consult the comprehensive study of Thomas Coı *and Use of Baptizein* (Grand Rapids, MI: Kregel Publı
5. In Leviticus 14:15, in the Septuagint (the Greek tra Old Testament) each of these words is used to indicat actions that they describe: pouring, sprinkling, and dı
6. A child's inherent standing before God (Matthew 1 sanctifying cover of a parent's faith (7:14) are to be trı keep children safe until they reach the necessary level opment where they can make the personal decision to sin (even as a future life path) toward faith in Christ.
7. See Everett Ferguson, *Baptism in the Early Church: . and Liturgy in the First Five Centuries* (Grand Rapids, 2013).
8. R. T. France, *The Gospel of Matthew*, in the New In mentary on the New Testament (Grand Rapids, MI:]
9. The word "for" (Greek *eis*) in Acts 2:38 indicates th the purpose of the forgiveness of sins. Some say "for" ı *previous faith* that sins are forgiven. But that is contraı The word "for" (Greek eis) in Acts 2:38 means *into*, lil

Recommended Reading

For Serious Bible Students

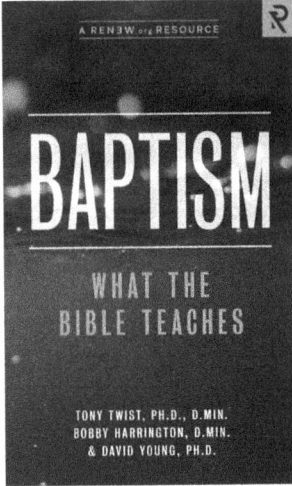

In-Depth Exploration for Preachers, Pastors, and Bible Scholars

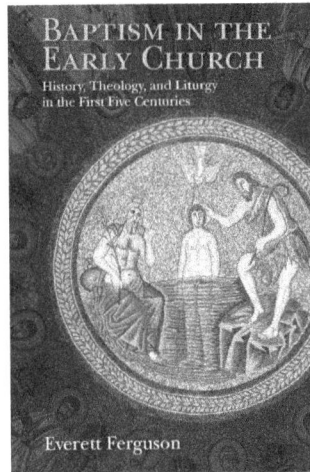

www.ingramcontent.com/pod-product-compliance
Lightning Source LLC
Chambersburg PA
CBHW062128040426
42337CB00044B/4386